THE HERMIT
SAYS GOODBYE

Also by Richard Teleky

FICTION

The Blue Hour

Winter in Hollywood

Pack Up the Moon

The Paris Years of Rosie Kamin

Goodnight, Sweetheart and Other Stories

NON-FICTION

Ordinary Paradise: Essays on Art and Culture

The Dog on the Bed: A Canine Alphabet

Hungarian Rhapsodies: Essays on Ethnicity, Identity and Culture

POETRY

The Hermit in Arcadia

The Hermit's Kiss

ANTHOLOGIES

The Exile Book of Canadian Dog Stories

The Oxford Book of French-Canadian Short Stories

THE HERMIT SAYS GOODBYE

RICHARD TELEKY

Publishers of Singular
Fiction, Poetry, Nonfiction, Translation, Drama and Graphic Books

Library and Archives Canada Cataloguing in Publication

Title: The hermit says goodbye / Richard Teleky.
Names: Teleky, Richard, 1946- author.
Description: Poems.
Identifiers: Canadiana (print) 2019014985X | Canadiana (ebook)
  20190149868 | ISBN 9781550968538 (softcover) |
  ISBN 9781550968545 (EPUB) | ISBN 9781550968552 (Kindle) |
  ISBN 9781550968569 (PDF)
Classification: LCC PS8589.E375 H465 2019 | DDC C811/.54—dc23

Copyright © Richard Teleky, 2019
Book design by Michael Callaghan
Typeset in Bembo and Birka fonts at Moons of Jupiter Studios
Cover painting *Abstract in Blue* (*Abstraction en bleu*), 1959,
  by Paul-Émile Borduas © estate Paul-Émile Borduas
Published by Exile Editions Ltd ~ www.ExileEditions.com
144483 Southgate Road 14 – GD, Holstein, Ontario, N0G 2A0
Printed and Bound in Canada by Marquis

We gratefully acknowledge the Canada Council for the Arts, the Government
of Canada, the Ontario Arts Council, and the Ontario Media Development
Corporation for their support toward our publishing activities.

 Conseil des Arts du Canada   Canada Council for the Arts   Canada

 ONTARIO ARTS COUNCIL / CONSEIL DES ARTS DE L'ONTARIO   Ontario / Ontario Media Development Corporation

Canadian sales representation:
The Canadian Manda Group, 664 Annette Street, Toronto ON, M6S 2C8
www.mandagroup.com 416 516 0911

North American and international distribution, and U.S. sales:
Independent Publishers Group, 814 North Franklin Street,
Chicago IL 60610 www.ipgbook.com toll free: 1 800 888 4741

In memory of

Priscila Uppal
(1974–2018)

Audrey King Wilson
(1947–2018)

I

II

III

What century is it outside?
—BORIS PASTERNAK

I

I'll stay young if I have to do it on one leg.
—WISŁAWA SZYMBORSKA

MARCH CLEAN-UP

Gathering me, you gather / your Self.
—ROBERT DUNCAN

Calling it mud season
gives the spring melt a panache
belied by the mess of it all.
Is that a new man on the horizon?
Robert Duncan would say yes.
I've been reading "The Torso"
and imagine a kiss or two
while watching my footprints
in the wet lawn, which can be
harmful to the compacted soil
underneath the melting snow.
The sun is now higher in the sky,
and since twelve units of snow
equals one of water, it matters
where you walk while checking out
the spring melt, before the world
undresses again and bodies
appear like the first snowdrops.

A WELL, TEARS

Quis dabit oculis nostris fontem lacrimarum?
                              —JEAN MOUTON (circa 1520)

What challenge drives the ochre-edged branches
beside New York's interstate, brownish gray bark
pulsing with the holy greens of ordinary time?

Easter Monday's a good start for a road trip,
yet a brief snow flurry, drifting over the northern
lake on my right, slows the way for half an hour.

"Who will give to our eyes a well of tears?"
sing radio monks in an old motet, voices spiraling
like the wet snowflakes against my windshield.

Is there an answer? When Augustine cried
"I took too long to fall in love with you, beauty
so ancient and so new," his aching crossed

the centuries and made me close my book,
as if nothing more need be said: Now,
trusting, you live however you can. So –

"Oregon!" I tell the dog, asleep in his kennel
on the front seat, adding it to "New Jersey"
and "Pennsylvania" and "Maine," license plates

from a childhood car-trip game I still play,
but now to keep my memory sharp and not,
as the states mount up, to exalt their spotting.

Once the snow stops a road-kill rabbit appears,
then the torn body of a decomposing deer.
Death will always be with us, sometimes swift,

often not, ancient yet new. I cannot fall in love
with it, no matter how I try. I object. I object
again and again, failing this starkest challenge.

RIPE PEACHES FROM
THE ORCHARD OF THE WARLORD

The orchard, we could imagine, is imaginary.
It's alive with insects that are born and die
in one day, and bats, skunks, even a rats' nest
or two. Think about that for a while, will you,

as I recall peach fuzz, smooth as the bald spot
on Grandpa's head, but pinkish-yellow – not gray –
with a sweet-sour taste, not tart exactly,
nor sugary, yet thick with August's promise.

"But Grandpa can't die," I once said during
one of his surgeries, or so I've been told.
"Who would mow the lawn?" The old soldier
drank like a fish and worked like a dog.

He made the plot in a neglected field next door,
cleared the brush, burned back poison ivy,
then planted whatever he liked: rows of tall corn
and, before I was born, five peach trees.

Forget about pies and jams, they came later.
Grandpa wanted the cycle of blossom
to fruit, and what happened next wasn't his bother.
He had a taste for satisfaction, not a sweet tooth.

The field garden was battle ground to him.
Wild rabbits, damn poison ivy returning,
those troublesome birds peeking at his crop,
of course late frosts, too much rain, you name it.

He didn't stand on guard, a scarecrow had that job,
only a broomstick with a worn white sheet draped
over a wood hangar, flapping with every breeze,
poor ragtag sentry, not noble, just makeshift.

How proud he was that a Hungarian farm boy
could serve as a U.S. Army corporal in Texas City,
Texas, where he drew in black ink the position sketch
of a town on Galveston Bay now hanging in my study.

His meticulous print records the Field Artillery Camp,
the Field Hospital, spaces marked for an oil refinery,
a wagon train, even a ballpark, but no peach trees.
None. Did he plot his field garden with such care?

Picked too soon, a peach is hard and sickly green,
too late, its fibrous mush sticks to your tongue,
but if the moment's ripe – like everything in life,
timing is all – you'll know fecund perfection.

Of course our garden was paved over with cement
half a century ago, for some school's parking lot,
its peach trees plowed under and buried like Grandpa.
The orchard, we could imagine, was imaginary.

MORPHINE COMA

In memory of Gitty Kretsch

Unpack the picnic hamper. Anita's in from Paris,
airplane weary but in time for the death watch.
Gitty's in the next room, mouth open, breathing hard,
unavailable for a lunch she would have liked –
cold cuts, deli rye and macaroons – but morphine's
    now her only nourishment.

On plates that once held homemade lemon squares
I set out store-bought rugelach, then glance
into the family room where she semi-sleeps
on a rented hospital bed. At eighty-six she takes along
the world of Jewish small farms in Madison, Ohio,
    not that fabled lower East Side.

Back then, with upward dreams, her parents
chose names from the British fancy class –
Lucille and Sylvia and Gloria – yet they morphed
into Lakie, Sorkie and Gitty for three Yiddish-Yankee
girls who marched into the future with the pains
    of Europe still in their blood.

Lakie, Sorkie and Gitty – the youngest – overnight
became so old, so old, it took their breath away.
Don't ask me to forget, sings Jacques Brel
on a CD Anita brought along, *don't ask,*
    don't ask, don't ask.

These women weren't mine. Still, memory's not
for the dead, they don't need it now, so conjure
the squawk of a chicken when its neck was wrung,
long Shabbos prayers and vile slurs, already
     what they heard is lost for good.

But I can touch the gold-rimmed china vase
Gitty once gave me to remember her by,
and it will always be hers as long as it's mine,
filled with summer delphinium or autumn mums
     and the short life of their own.

FLOODPLAIN

If it were possible to crawl
    between old layers of paint
to see the room – never mind the world –
    through Sherwin Williams' Linen
with its hint of ochre warming up
    the white, down to the next layer
of soiled beige, to the dull chalky blue
    of a dank November afternoon

before hitting plaster, now damply silken
    from a broken water pipe above
but glistening like the antique walls
    of some Venetian palazzo, say
Peggy Guggenheim's, where paintings
    could be hung with flair against
the rotting patina of mother-of-pearl,
    pink to apricot to mouldy gray,

and so soft to touch you'd think
    of a beloved naked back rubbed
with fancy sunscreen, only then,
    only after the cracks began and
blistering rose to demand attention,
    a few pocks at first but soon a crowd,
audience to the great damage rushing
    water can make when walled in

or forced to spread over parquet floors,
    oriental carpets, a pile of books
stacked beside the closet, a new pair
    of shoes never meant for wading
across a stream, though well made
    with fine leather soles, the walls hued
in shadows, and weeks ahead for
    shape-shifting as the drying begins,

lilac splotches belonging in a museum
    on an action painter's best canvas,
still I might want to sink deeper
    into the concrete, where water
took its own course, as if it knew
    its mind and mine could follow
with only the emotions well known
    to stone, paint, or drywall.

WATCHING *L'ATALANTE*

00:00

On a Friday morning in February
the movie bride gingerly crosses
my TV and steps onto an old barge.
As grease smudges white satin
the handsome young groom –
Jean, officially – consoles her
with kisses. Who are they to me?
Yet the soupy whine of an accordion
makes me long for a wet home.
Voilà! the bride says. Years ago,
she confesses, his face came to her
in a pool of water: match that.
Later Jean, shirtless, seeks her face
in the laundry tub. "I wanted to see
you there," he teases. "You'll believe me
when it's for real," she says, caressing
his shoulders, eyes turned up to a place
outside the screen (such bliss) while
I watch the light splash on his back
in lush black-and-white shadows.

09:47

Fog, river smoke, a clanging bell,
these are Jean's world. Below,
Juliette follows Paris fashion

by radio: berets are back in style.
Le père Jules, Jean's old barge
hand, must resent all the kissing.
He has no soft bride like Juliette
and just one choice: to leave
or befriend her as an accomplice.
What good is love if it isn't
on display? Now he can only watch
or warm himself beside the cat.
He has seen Shanghai, San Francisco,
the bushmen of Australia, and
Yokohama – so what? A body
can match any foreign land.

27:34

Bodies – bright puppets, no
more than the mementos Jules
displays from a life on water:
a music-box man from Caracas,
Javanese marionettes, two
human hands preserved in a jar,
these fascinate the bride, so
Jules strips to his waist and shows
off his tattoos. Seeing him, Jean
smashes a few souvenirs.
"Are you crazy?" cries the bride.
Yes, he is. He has only his muscles,
no San Francisco or Singapore.
He knows you love with your body.

The fogs, mists, dark river nights
have taught him that much, even if
his best suit smells of moth balls.

29:40

Then Paris! And more water –
the Seine with its docks, locks,
canals. *Infamous, wonderful city,*
Jules calls through a fog horn.
In bed, Juliette reaches for Jean –
"Oh, it's you," she says coyly –
and while they form a ball of flesh
she adds, "I dreamed you went away
and left me." Muscles do count.
Paris, Paris, sings Jules, *You
great bewitcher*. But he knows
that muscles are the true draw,
everyone in Paris looking for them.
On shore next morning, the couple
sport their love in the streets.
Moules, frites, vin; the future
is everywhere. Does Juliette care
if her groom smells of moth balls?
Not while dancing with a stranger
as Jean watches from their table –
he can match *those* muscles
any day – so he stops their fun,
reclaims the bride, returns her
to the wharf, the barge, the marriage.

53:36

Yet Juliette's dance partner
follows with the new scarf
she's forgotten – her souvenir,
though not as rare as a jar
of pickled hands – and tempts
her to a night on the town.
She accepts the scarf but
Jean clears out the intruder
before pacing on deck.

59:34

What's going in Juliette's mind?
After midnight she heads ashore,
leaving an unmade bed (that trope).
Jean can't know she wants only an hour
of sweet talk and window shopping.
He steers the barge onward without her.

1:03:15

Morning: the wharf's empty.
Oh to be loved, in his arms,
not by herself in a forlorn
City of Lights. Little's left
for the groom but checkers
with Jules and cigarette solace.
"Electricity," asks Jules, as he sets

out to fix the broken phonograph,
"do you know what it is?"

1:10:14

Wearing his street clothes, Jean
jumps into the river, swims deep,
as if in search of Juliette: a mermaid
mirage, white bridal gown beckoning.

1:14:02

Alone, Juliette removes her stockings,
sleeps fitfully in a strange bed.
Alone, Jean turns on their pillows,
twists, caresses his arm pit, as if
a trace of the soft bride might be
hiding there – a shocking moment
for 1934, all things considered.
She rubs her neck, his hand glides
over his chest, his nipple, a plump dark
aureole, she clasps her luminescent
right breast, lost in absent flesh.

1:16:19

Le Havre, finally. After docking Jean
runs to the beach, stares at the Atlantic.
He forgets to shave – why bother?
He forgets to work – what for?

The barge no longer matters
with all claims of flesh pressing:
Juliette must be found. Of course
he succeeds, this being well-scripted.
Jean shaves, washes, then waits.
Juliette returns, flesh falls on flesh
and the barge moves again through
glistening water, a silver pattern of light.

Jean Dasté, *Jean*, died in 1994.
Dita Parlo, *Juliette*, in 1971.
Michel Simon, *le père Jules*, in 1975.
Jean Vigo, *réalisateur*, 1934.

Outside my window snow falls.
I think of your body – your neck
and shoulders, stomach, thighs – its
own fine City of Light. When will you
come to me, my bride, my groom?

I WILL NOT WRITE [YOUR NAME]

i.
There is no story
to thwarted longing,
a premature grave.

ii.
Dig another hole.
Settle in, alone, with
the worm's well-being.

iii.
Sometimes, yes. But
not always. Yet sometimes.
And all too often.

iv.
What are we meant to be?
I don't know you but I should
know enough to let this go.

v.
Unavailable. – Almost.
Desirable. – Almost.
Absurd. – Naturally.

vi.
Language has to break down.
I am repelled by this hole,
a familiar one beckoning.

vii.
Still, smelling defeat,
I crouch beside it, waiting
for the fever to break.

viii.
If you give me this poem,
what of it? Gratitude?
As always, time will tell.

ix.
And what does it tell?
Something wonderful
didn't happen. So what?

x.
The air is dry.
You are now paper.
Put down the pen.

ADVICE, UNSOLICITED, TO COUPLES

Hear ye all husbands, wives, partners,
cohorts and significant others:

No matter how unhappy you are –
bored, discontented, perhaps only restless –
no matter how satisfied, loving, gregarious,
think twice before you go into the world
ensconced, then think once again.
You give each other a base of well-being,
fragile as it may be, with the *egoism*
à deux D. H. Lawrence lamented.
You are not safe for this world,
you believe yourself to be kind,
but when you reach out in friendship
your hand is always set to draw back.
Go home to each other, *hurry now!*
and look to your love with gratitude.

AN HOUR AGO

Woke to a child crying out in the night.
    No, I thought, it's a wailing cat.

Why has it taken my door for its own?
    Why will this April snow not stop?

Perhaps I should follow it into the street.
    There must be an answer. Listen again:

It's not a cat, and it's not outside, only my
    wheezing, now the sound of a poem.

II

Expect God evenly in all things.
—MEISTER ECKHART

PERSEPHONE ON A TREE STUMP

For Peter Perenyi

You called the old head
by an ancient name as it rests
there atilt, lips open to the day,
armless – bodyless, in fact –
no Hide and Seek for her,
just morning sun and shadows,
evening shade, a forelock
(once red?) faded now to gray,
in some lights white, moon-
streaked by deathless bright
hypnotic gleam or glimmer
of tales we offer to each other.
While there's still time ahead –
eyes unseeing, shut – she knows
no reason, good or bad, to bother
with a thought for you or me.
Should I have asked what she
was made of? Dreams, perhaps.
Or for her origin, and how a head
came to this resting place?
But we were forging on, atilt
with death, not an antique brain.

AT THE BUTLER INSTITUTE OF AMERICAN ART, WITH JOAN MITCHELL AND RENNIE

Blue gray yellow violet
                              green.

Over marble floors, I carry you.

The canvas wall is bigger than the world.
I want to walk into it with you,
through the throbbing colors,

    you, who should not
        be here, are:
    a choice made for me
    that let me be us.

    Together we might walk
    into the blue, the green –
    a landscape, her memory.

Brush strokes this way and that,
on top of each other,
                              ascending,
                                        decending.

There's red and black, too – a sunflower swirl.

And we are here now,
for only this while,
in a forbidden space.

Your paws do not touch the floor
though an invitation's been made:
   "You can put him down."

But I want to keep you safe,

I want to look at the walls
and know you're secure in my arms,
                near my heart.

DIGGING

How the roses pass.
—James Schuyler

The hole must be as deep as the pot
and twice as wide, or Gertrude Jekyll –
rose, not woman – will have trouble
settling in. So I dig, and after ten inches
hit clay, thick and red, with shards
of glass and even a rusted railway tie.
Digging in Surrey, what did she unearth?
Jekyll's the ghost in this new bush –
a strong damask scent – or so the tag says,
but it doesn't claim that ghosts can grow
in gardens if you know where to look.
Still, I shouldn't expect well-wishing
from a green shade, who would rather
be up here in the air, me in her place.

THE FIELD NEXT DOOR

Thick snow heavies branch and bough
in a black-and-white snapshot where
Mother models a new raccoon coat. Look:
see her pleasure, the Depression's still
on yet she's bought the coat herself,
if she'd shot the creatures she couldn't
feel more entitled to bask in their pelts.
Who held the camera? Not Grandma, no.
Then her sister, or a boyfriend whose name
I've never heard. Mother's boots are planted
on a snowdrift, rubber soles with fur
ankle trim. There appear to be animal
tracks on the ground, perhaps a rabbit
has run off, disturbed by human trespass.

SEPARATION ANXIETY

For Toby

A ruby King Charles denied Crufts
or Westminster for a blaze of white
that begins above his coal-black nose

and flares for half an inch between
his eyes, then meanders to his forehead
in a forbidden streak, as if some god's

fingertip had stroked him there and left
that glowing print, unaware it banished
him to a barn, for nine months, as unfit.

And in those months alone he licked
his kennel walls, cowered at thunderstorms
and waited for me without knowing what

he waited for. Once rescued, the damage
had been done. "You know I'll be back,"
I say, assuming I will, yet he barks

in desperation if I move to leave. "What more
do you want?" The answer's clear enough:
he only wants to be the center of my eye.

MEMORY SONG

Translated from Pierre Morency's
Le chant de ma mémoire

A cat scratches the bark,
of a forcefully risen tree.

Sunlight hits the window,
a beam arrives and pierces me.

Monsieur Madame stroll out together;
small steps ring down the lane.

Remarks exit from houses;
Folks dress their memories.

A tree arches over the garden;
The cat ascends beneath its leaves.

Where is the nest of my childhood?

BAKING ICELANDIC BROWN BREAD

For Betty Jane Wylie

You work the dough as I watch,
first rising over, the touch – or feel
of it – crucial, with an elasticity
unavailable to the eye alone.
"Never put yeast in cold water,"
you warn, a pause in kneading,
"or its enzymes won't bloom."
And it's best to use water left
from cooking potatoes, there's
extra leaven to raise the bread.
Remember how fragile yeast is,
like the first draft of a poem.

[HUNTINGTON] BEACH

The shoreline has names.
People try to enforce them:

it's *this* park, not *that* one.
But what good is a name?

I come here to escape them.
Of course the water doesn't care.

Why should it? So much older,
it has absorbed all the names.

6:20 A.M.

The sunroom has ten windows, one door,
a single bed. The dog sits by my feet, trembling,

he jerks his head left to right, then right to left,
he lowers it as if expecting to be hit, smacked hard,

looks up at me, eyes filled with desperation,
stares at the door – cocked head – hunches forward,

jumps down to the floor, turns to face the space
beneath the bed, curls himself into a ball.

It's been raining half an hour, an early summer
downpour – no thunder, though – just pounding rain,

stabbing in staccato, slashing against the panes.
There's a moment of silence before relentless

new waves hit, yet to me most comforting
as I read a new translation of Chekhov

by lamplight, while the dog hears horrors
in the rain I haven't fathomed. Another silence.

The dog looks up blankly: *Is it over now?*
But no, not yet, the storm starts up again.

His eyes glaze over, he doesn't seem to ask,
Can't you stop it? He won't count on me.

What's in the rain for him? Nazis at the door,
the NKVD stalking Isaac Babel in the middle

of the night, some mad dog's pursuit? Mind's
terror is so great he takes no comfort from

my stroking hand, a soft "Good boy." Suddenly,
vast ominous stillness. We both sit and wait

as I set my book aside. Insistent drops no longer
tap even their lightest. We continue to wait.

BEWARE

Two young guys from Miskolc sand
and varnish and buff my parquet floors

when one cuts his hand. I'm quick
to offer Band-Aids and Polysporin.

We stand together in the bathroom
and look down at the raw red gash

across his thumb. *Fiám*, I nearly say
in his language, a too-familiar word,

my boy, my son. You must be more
careful, you're overworked, drained

by the local vampires who call
themselves landlords and entrepreneurs

and draw every drop of blood better
than a Transylvanian monster can.

AKEDAH

To kill your son
is to kill yourself –

to kill your father
means a prison term.

Long ago, a young man
dubbed this a paradox.

Fearing knives and pens,
the innocent signed

his book "Victor Eremita":
Victorious Hermit.

Old Abe lacked enough
courage for solitude.

Unshadowed, the victory
matters only to you.

MR. SARASTRO'S 6 STEPS TO WISDOM

1. Forget everything you've heard about me. Nothing is
   what it seems.

2. Better burn than marry. My ex-, Queenie – the
   shrew of all shrews – controlled both night and day.
   Even money couldn't buy off her rages.

3. But never masturbate. That pretty boy with the picture,
   head over heels from a cheap image, worked himself
   into a tizzy. Scratch an itch long enough and you'll
   end up with a wound.

4. And watch out for nature – all those rocks and trees
   and flowers, a trap. The bird you catch can pluck
   your eyes out.

5. Beware melting pleas. A good girl, Pam, but always that
   same smile: Save me, save me! Just find the right pill.
   Imagine wards of bliss, people asleep, cozily drugged.
   The only thing to worry about is bedsores.

6. Everyone has a story – heroes, too. Like music, they
   make emotions you don't need.

N IS FROM INDEX

Found poem from Fanny Howe

Next time I'll travel by dream
No more cinders, the cellar water is iced over
Nothing in life is so exciting
Now a daring blue heron
Nuns, monks and swamis

"DOG BEACH," WE CALL IT

North of Malibu
M. sits in the shade
    with pug and spaniel,
while nearby L. bakes, oil-
    slathered, and I
wander Sycamore Cove as
    the tide comes in
foaming, the orgasmic sea
    churning around
my feet at the rocks' edge –
    the air scented with
mussels that cling to forms
    shaped by air and water
until they resemble jade
    sponges, moon craters,
or a Chinese ink painting.
    This tidal pool, streaked
with black slicks in Pollack
    patterns – gray, brown,
the faintest of blues – as
    sun hits water diamonds
now breaking ankle high.
    My face burns, eyes
too, and it's easy to ignore
    the Pacific Coast Highway
at my back, or a low plane
    overhead, the ocean roar
predictably pulsing, a lover

who taunts without promise
of satisfaction or peace. Die
     in me, it beckons,
the scent of Coppertone wafting
     a strong hint of sex,
like incoming tidal waves
     remoulding themselves.
Later, on a red-eye flight home,
     I try to forget the moment
when it seemed the sea's rumble
     might stop for good.

HIS LAST PALETTE

What use would I be, deprived of painting.
　　　　　　　　　　—GEORGES BRAQUE

raw umber
burnt umber
raw sienna
burnt sienna
yellow ochre
lamp black
vine black
bone black
ultramarine
orange-yellow
antimony yellow

III

Tell them my eyes / stayed open.
—Federico García Lorca

EUDAIMONIA

Before – until – I was born surely
I never knew suffering or pain
because I never knew consciousness.
But I also never knew pleasure –
what kind of trade-off is that?
Yet life brought the future of the past.
What can I now be seeking?
Sheer chivalry, like ambivalence,
remains a banal guise: the paradox
of myself and yourself. We meet
in this poem for a brief while
but do we meet with goodwill?
Only if you say so. Perhaps.

DAWN

The mourning doves are back again,
    off an old Chinese scroll.

A wild rabbit chomps clover,
    with no regard for me.

Neanderthals could start fires,
    the morning paper claims,

and afternoon means a thunderstorm.
    Will there be fireflies tonight?

ANOTHER AUGUST

Despite the brutal sun
day after day after day,
a rose wants to open,
wants to be, for its moment,
inexhaustible – free.

As I watch this summer
guest, alive to the burning air,
green worm and blackening leaf,
there's no escape for us
from autumn's grief.

Cancer for one pal, old-age
madness for another,
chemo and chemo again,
pills, tubes, a catheter,
yet still that sun burns on.

Prospero said "Enough!" –
the magic has to end.
The rose will pale and die,
the sky will darken soon,
our time for burning through.

URN

For R

Without you to care for
I need a new start.
Where to place the ad?
Professional mourner,
no fee. I'll lead any slow
march to a grave site,
then weep endless tears.
No one need know
they're only for you.

MOURNING

It's hard to imagine
any possible silence:
think of the word's red *m*,
or its muddy brown *g*.
Mourning's a swirl
of repetition rushing
       nowhere.

CHOPIN'S LAST FUNERAL

As a final request, Frederic Chopin (1810-49)
asked that his heart be entombed in Poland.

Smuggled out of Paris in a jar of cognac, it was
exhumed many times, and once guarded by Nazis.

On April 14, 2014, it was buried again,
in secret, in Warsaw's Holy Cross Church.

He fed on grief while it fed on him
as moonlit notes blew across his pages
like October leaves in a whip of wind.

How much of what he did did he understand?
The notes kept him alive but sucked out life.
The notes poured fast, indifferent to grieving:
a nightingale's cry, a rose dropping petals,
tubercle bacillus amok. Still notes kept coming.

People told tales about him, jealous or reverent.
He didn't bother to listen, an eagle alone
swallowing all the notes, beating his wings to them.
Pages blew across his table, notes splattered the pages.

But once the notes stopped his hand fell aside,
someone closed his piano — would wormwood set in?

The eagle at his summit took a breath, then another,
ready to plunge down through his past present future
into the world in himself. The heart as metaphor
hasn't pumped a drop of blood for eons now.

REFUGE: EVER THIS DAY

*You are the last person in the twentieth century
who still has a guardian angel.*

—Magda Szabó

Angels, I've read, will gather
all the signs of the zodiac,
tie them together and bonfire
the bundle, a warning that time's
finally done for good.

At the hour of escape, if you
had to put all your possessions
into a cart before walking slowly
through the wind, rain, and snow,
what would you take?

And would you stop to eat a stew
of thistles and wild honey, choking
on dust? Or say to a fellow traveler,
"Do you know if the angels in heaven
suffer from low intelligence?"

DIES IRAE

Hermit, absolve our sins…
—GUILLAUME APOLLINAIRE

In place of lunch, let's walk
under the new wolf moon,
taking its measure slowly.

Of course we'll have bad days,
many bad days, but it's better
to bear them directly in face off.

My pants need pressing now.
I can't sense your body against mine.
There's no time left for pretending.

READY...

After sixty years it's almost time to sell the family house,
my other home, just a red brick box circa 1947.

From every corner I can watch a high-definition past
with that naïve kid lost in yearning, Tebaldi and Bergonzi

the other play bohemians in the room. There's *Tom Jones*
on the night stand and sexy Albert Finney dashing about

in his nightshirt in my muddled head. 1963? Pick a year –
any year – and every room opens onto moments like the time

I struggled to roll the right French *R* the way Greco
could when she crooned "*Parlez-moi d'amour*" or I sat

memorizing German declensions (*kann nicht vergessen*)
with Christmas wrapping paper on the floor and someone

telling of a doctor's bad report. Now I should practice
locking the door one last time, then passing on the key.

CLOWN OF DUST

From above your basin peered the Noh
Mask of a hermit with brown rice-grain teeth
And close-cropped silver hair.
A clown of dust...

—JAMES MERRILL

When the face above the basin
Looks up with fixed dismay:
Who's that? you say *Who's that?*
That's you the morning offers back.
Okay, not really silver cropped,
Just gray-streaked mousy brown,
Though Colgate Whitening works
Its glow on aging chompers.
Take it or leave it – be quick!
You have to decide for yourself,
Pretend to know where you are now,
The time for changing drama gone.
Yet hermits clown for better things
Than final dust and all it has to bring.

HERMITAGE APPLICATION

Wanted: A Resident Hermit for Solothurn, Switzerland.
Along with acting as caretaker and sacristan, responsibilities
include interaction with the many visitors.

—THE WALL STREET JOURNAL

My face is rose-red,
my hands are grass green,
my eyes seek the blue.

Don't expect a solemn bow
from me, not once, not twice,
and never three times.

If you would like to stroll
through my grounds – my life –
you'd better think again.

Here, I'll hold your hands,
then bind them with twine.
The night air's sweet in heliotrope.

Why have you bothered to come?
I didn't buy colored lights for you.
Can't you feel the air vibrate?

Cultivate indifference to yourself.
True needs are few. Find a place
to eat, to sleep, to defecate.

See? You only need repetition.
Your visit must never happen again.
Live right and the world's a hermitage.

GOODBYE

Do I mean it?
Can I mean it?
    I'll try.

A hermit doesn't say no
        to the world,
        but yes.

A hermit doesn't say
        I love you,
        but I love.

You and the world are present
        at every moment,
        only more alive

to my eye than you
        have ever been
        before.

I know you to be alive
        for yourself
        alone,

your own life your heart,
    the place you honor
    above all.

So I say yes to you,
    to you and the world: be
    whatever you wish,

the world may even go along,
    and of course I say
    yes.

NOTES AND ACKNOWLEDGEMENTS

My thanks, once again, to Barry Callaghan, Chris Doda, Anna Graham, Jason Guriel, Nora Shulman, Teresa Stratas and Priscila Uppal, for thoughtful readings and comments. And a special nod of appreciation to Michael Callaghan, for his fine design work and goodwill.

❊

The epigraph for *The Hermit Says Goodbye* comes from Boris Pasternak's "About These Poems," first published in his influential 1921 collection *My Sister—Life*.

The epigraph for Part I is from "Likeness" by Wisława Szymborska, from *Poems New and Collected, 1957-1997*, translated by Stanislaw Baranczak and Claire Cavanagh (A Harvest Book/Harcourt Inc., 1998).

Lines from "The Torso, Passages 18 " are from *Robert Duncan Selected Poems*, edited by Robert J. Bertholf (New Directions, 1997).

Regarding "A Well, Tears": Jean Mouton's "Missa Dictes moy toutes voz pensées," performed by the Tallis Scholars, is available on CD from Gimell Records. The lines from Augustine's *Confessions* are from Sarah Ruden's translation (Modern Library, 2017).

L'Atalante (1934), directed by Jean Vigo, is available on DVD from Criterion.

The epigraph for Part II is attributed to the fourteenth-century German mystic and philosopher Meister Eckhart.

The exhibition of Joan Mitchell's paintings was held at the Butler Institute of American Art, in Youngstown, Ohio, in the summer of 2012.

The epigraph for "Digging" comes from James Schuyler's "The Morning of the Poem" in his *Collected Poems* (Farrar, Straus and Giroux, 1993).

"Le chant de ma mémoire" is from Pierre Morency's *Grand Fanal: poèmes et proses* (Boréal, 2018). One of Quebec's leading poets, Morency is the author of more than a dozen books.

"Akedah" refers to Søren Kierkegaard and to the story of Abraham and Isaac in Genesis 22. See Joakim Garff's *Søren Kierkegaard: A Biography*, translated by Bruce H. Kirmmse (Princeton University Press, 2005).

"Mr. Sarastro's 6 Steps to Wisdom" refers to characters from Mozart's last opera *The Magic Flute*.

The five lines of the found poem "N is from Index" come from the first-line index of Fanny Howe's *Selected Poems*, published by the University of California Press, 2000.

For Braque's last palette, see Alex Danchev's *Georges Braque: A Life* (Arcade, 2005).

The epigraph for Part III comes from Lorca's poem "From Here" in *Poet in Spain: Federico García Lorca*, translated by Sarah Arvia (Alfred A. Knopf, 2017).

The epigraph for "Refuge: Ever This Day" comes from Magda Szabó's novel *Iza's Ballad* (New York Review Books, 2016), originally published in 1963 and translated by George Szirtes.

The epigraph for "Dies Irae" comes from Guillaume Apollinaire's poem "The Hermit" in *Alcools: Poems 1898-1913*, translated by William Meredith (Anchor Books, 1965). Stanza two of "Dies Irae" includes a remark from Gertrude Stein's essay "A Picture of Occupied France," first published in the *Atlantic Monthly* in 1940.

In "Ready...," the reference to Renata Tebaldi and Carlo Bergonzi is to their classic 1959 recording of Puccini's *La Boheme*. Tony Richardson's film adaptation of *Tom Jones*, starring Albert Finney, was originally released in late 1963.

The advertisement for a hermit first appeared in the Swiss Catholic weekly *Katholisches Kirchenblatt* and was later reprinted in a *Wall Street Journal* article, "Wanted: Hermit, Must be People Person," on June 19, 2014.

The lines that open "Clown of Dust" come from James Merrill's "The Book of Ephraim" in *The Changing Light of Sandover* (Alfred A. Knopf, 2013).

❁

And, finally, my appreciation to the journals and anthology that first published some of the poems in this collection:

EXILE (ELQ) – "Chopin's Last Funeral," "I'll Not Write [Your Name]" and "Ripe Peaches from the Orchard of the Warlord"

New Quarterly – "Another August," "6:20 A.M."

Partisan – "Beware"

Queen's Quarterly – "Floodplain"

Windsor Review – "Baking Icelandic Brown Bread," "Clown of Dust," "Digging," "The Field Next Door" and "Persephone on a Tree Trunk"

and

I Found it at the Movies: An Anthology of Film Poems, edited by Ruth Roach Pierson (Toronto: Guernica, 2014) – "Watching *L'Atalante*"

NOTE ON THE AUTHOR

Richard Teleky is a Professor Emeritus (Humanities) and Senior Scholar of York University, in Toronto. His books include two collections of poems, *The Hermit's Kiss* (2006) and *The Hermit in Arcadia* (2011); four novels – *The Paris Years of Rosie Kamin*, which received the Ribalow Prize (U.S.) for the best novel of 1999, *Pack Up the Moon*, *Winter in Hollywood* and *The Blue Hour*, and a collection of short fiction, *Goodnight, Sweetheart and Other Stories*; and three works of non-fiction – *Hungarian Rhapsodies: Essays on Ethnicity, Identity and Culture*, *The Dog on the Bed: A Canine Alphabet*, a study of the human/dog bond, and most recently *Ordinary Paradise: Essays on Art and Culture*; he has also edited two anthologies: *The Oxford Book of French Canadian Short Stories* and *The Exile Book of Canadian Dog Stories*. Teleky's poems, essays and short fiction have appeared in journals and anthologies in Canada and the United States. His website is: richardteleky.com.